worship BAND PLAY-ALONG

BASS EDITION *Volume 3*

How Great Is Our God

T0081523

Recorded and produced by Jim Reith at BeatHouse Music, Milwaukee, WI

Lead Vocals by Tonia Emrich and Jim Reith
Background Vocals by Jim Reith and Janna Wolf
Guitars by Joe Gorman
Bass by Chris Kringel
Keyboard by Kurt Cowling
Drums by Del Bennett

ISBN 978-1-4234-1724-8

HAL•LEONARD® CORPORATION
7777 W. BLUEMOUND RD. P.O. BOX 13819 MILWAUKEE, WI 53213

Visit Hal Leonard Online at
www.halleonard.com

Above All

Words and Music by Paul Baloche and Lenny LeBlanc

wis-dom _ and all _ the ways _ of man, _____ You were here _ be-fore _ the world _ be-gan.

A-bove all _ king - doms, a-bove all _ thrones, a-bove all _

won - ders the world _ has ev-er known, _ a-bove all wealth and treas - ures of _ the earth, _

_____ there's no way to meas - ure what _ You're worth.

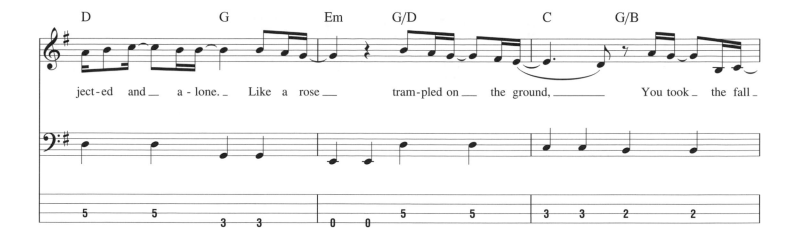

F Tag

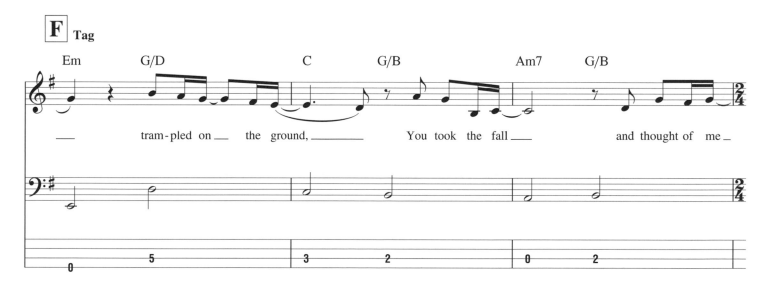

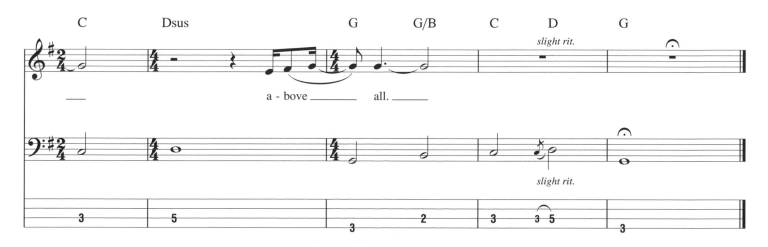

7

Beautiful Savior
(All My Days)
Words and Music by Stuart Townend

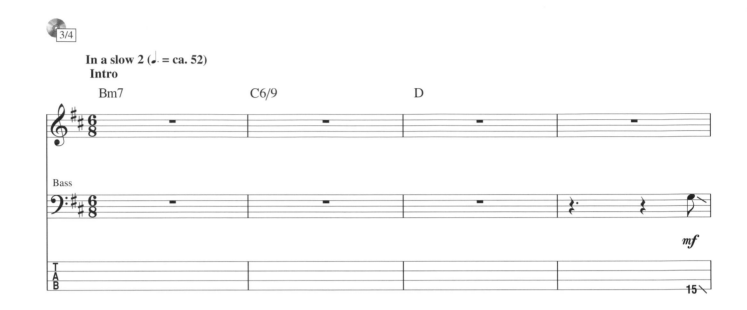

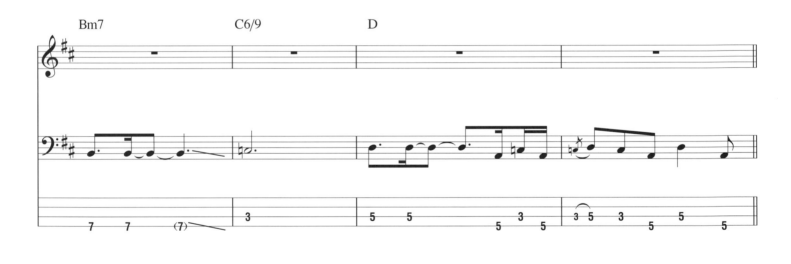

A **Verse 1**

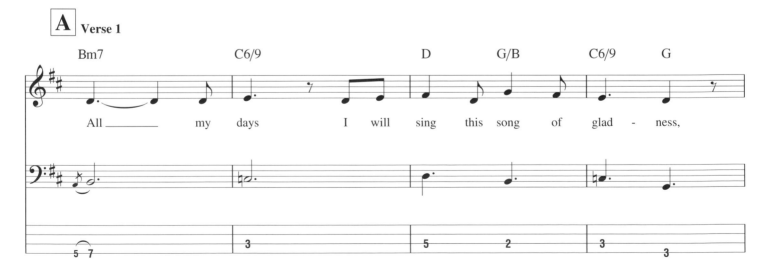

All _____ my days I will sing this song of glad - ness,

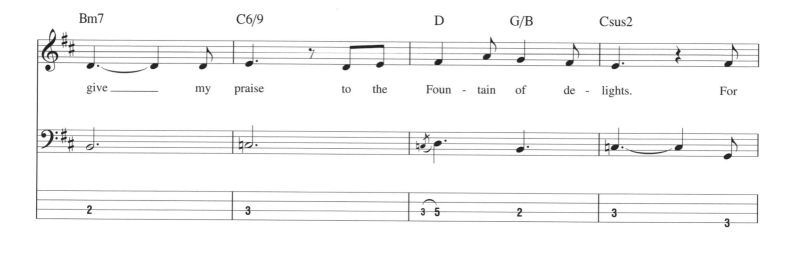

B Verse 2

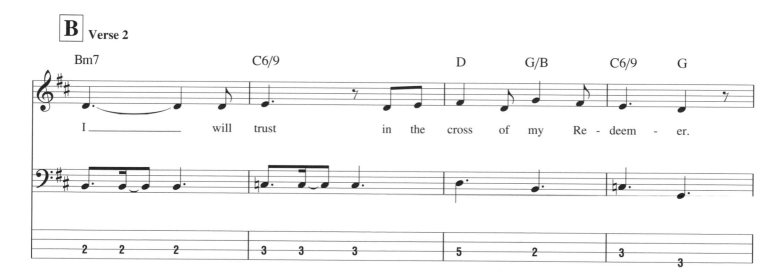

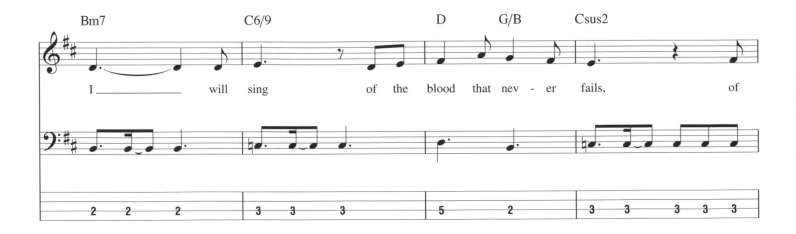

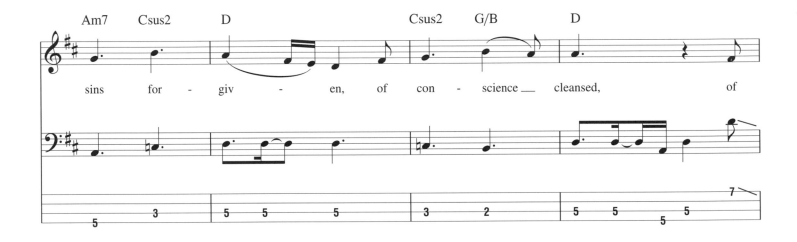

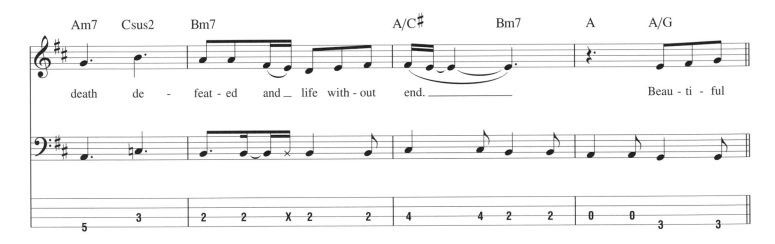

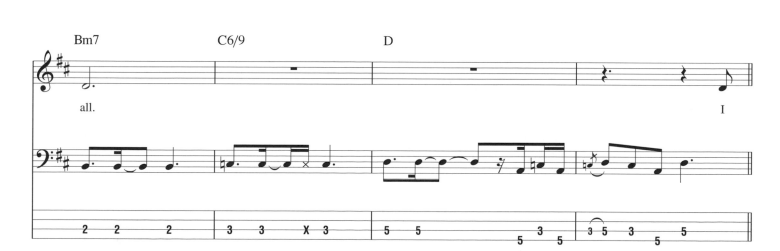

D Verse 3

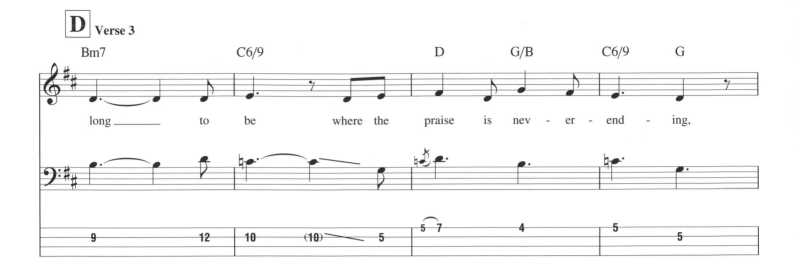

long _____ to be where the praise is nev-er-end - ing,

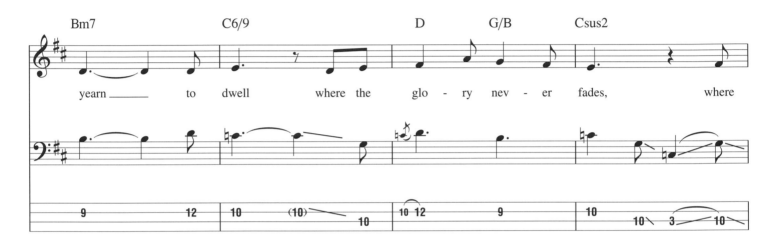

yearn _____ to dwell where the glo-ry nev-er fades, where

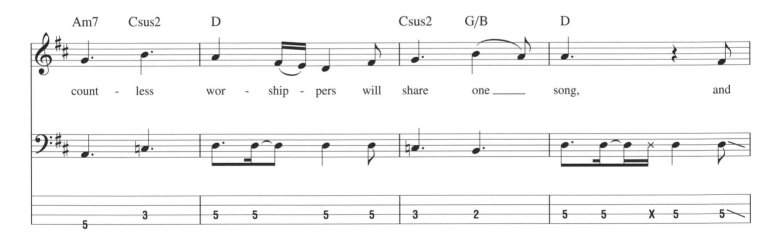

count - less wor - ship - pers will share one _____ song, and

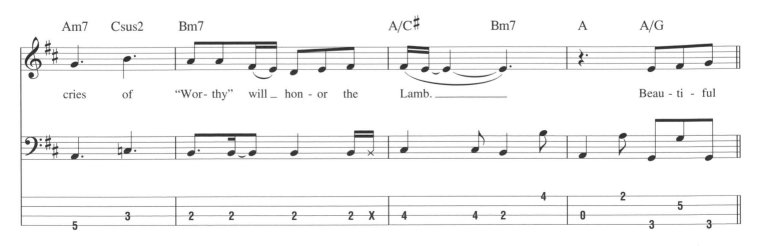

cries of "Wor-thy" will _ hon - or the Lamb. _____ Beau-ti-ful

12

champion, and You reign, You _____ reign. Beau-ti-ful

F Chorus

Sav - ior, _____ Won-der-ful Coun - sel - or, clothed in

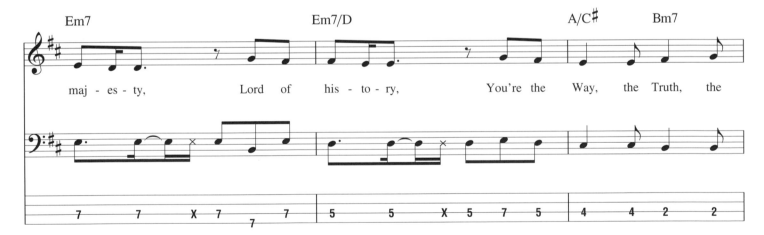

maj - es - ty, Lord of his - to - ry, You're the Way, the Truth, the

Life. Star of the Morn - ing, _____ glo - rious in

ho - li - ness,   You're the   Ris - en One,   heav - en's

cham - pi - on,   and You reign,   You _____ reign o - ver _ all, _____

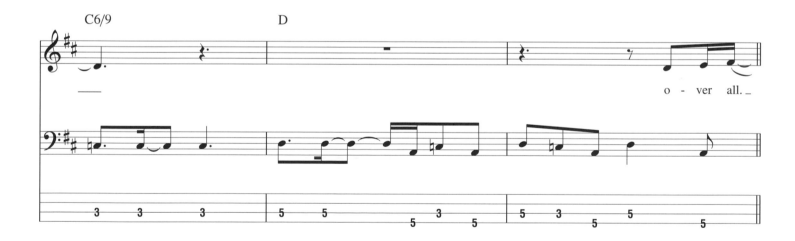

o - ver all. _

Tag

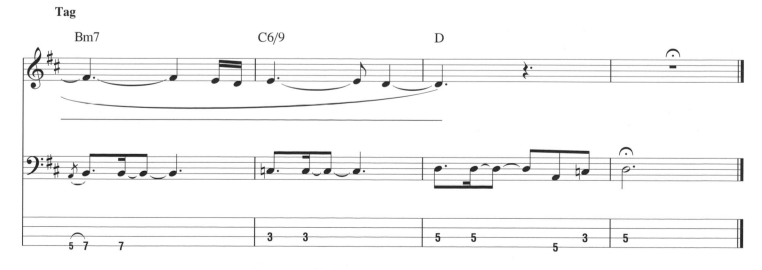

Days of Elijah

Words and Music by Robin Mark

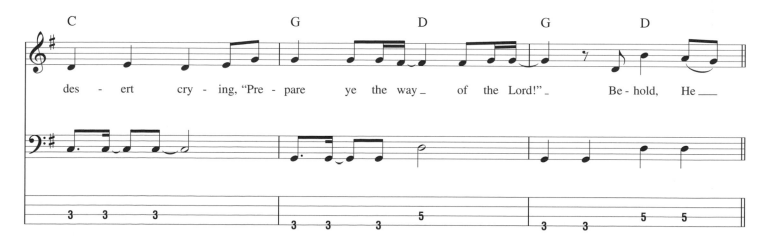

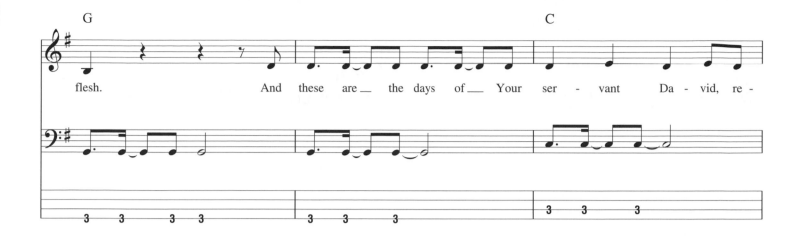

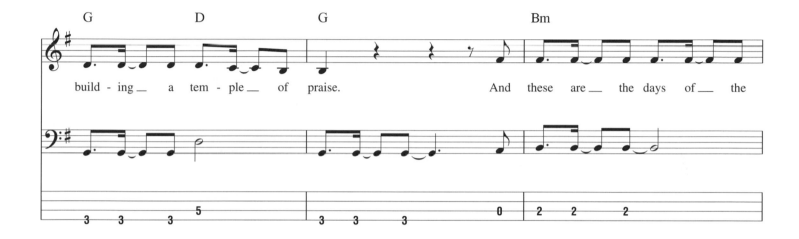

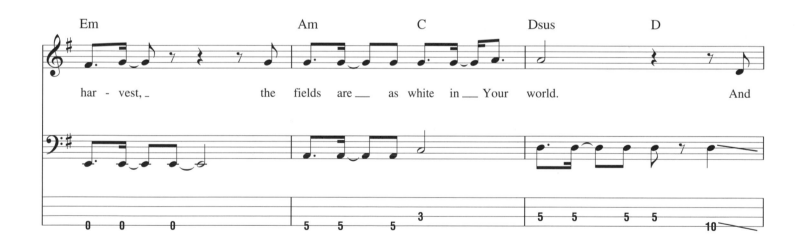

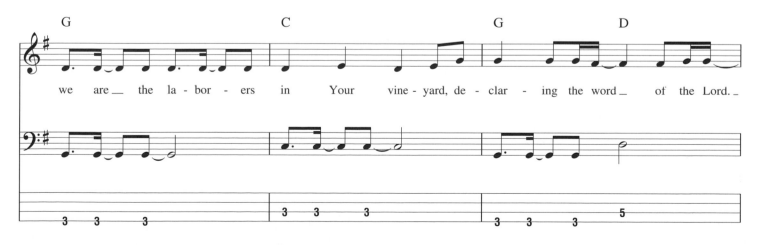

D Chorus

Be-hold, He __ comes, rid-ing on the clouds, __ shin-ing like the sun __

at the trum-pet call. Lift your __ voice, it's the year of Ju - bi - lee, __

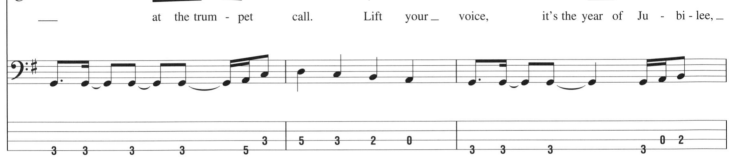

and out of Zi-on's hill sal - va - tion __ comes. Be-hold, He __

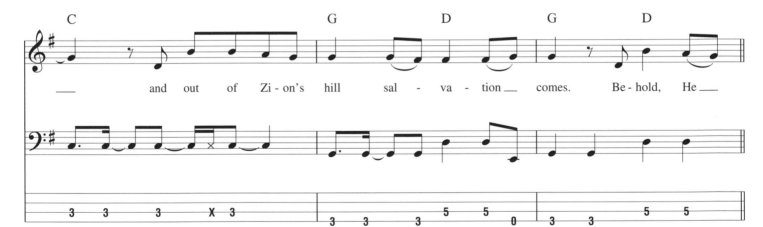

E Chorus

comes, rid-ing on the clouds, __ shin-ing like the sun __ at the trum-pet call. Lift your __

How Great Is Our God

Words and Music by Chris Tomlin, Jesse Reeves and Ed Cash

24

great _____ is our God. ___ All will see __ how great, how great __

___ is our God. _____

E **Bridge**

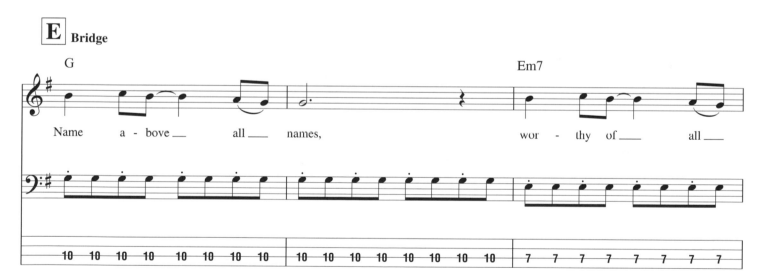

Name a - bove __ all __ names, wor - thy of __ all __

praise. My heart will sing: _____ How great _____ is our God! __

He's the Name a - bove___ all___

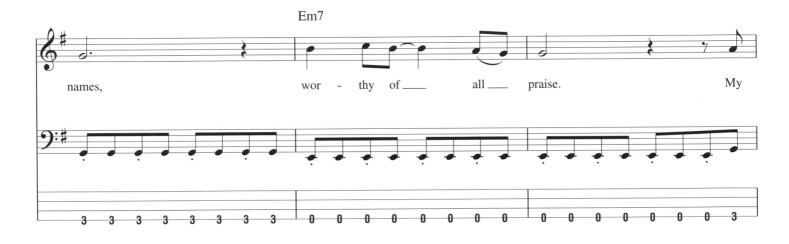

names, wor - thy of ___ all ___ praise. My

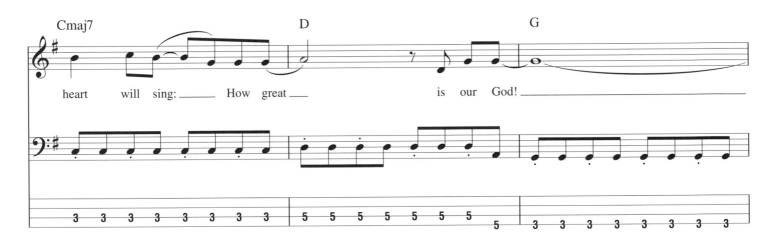

heart will sing:___ How great ___ is our God! ___

F **Chorus**

___ How great ___ is our God. ___ Sing with me, ___ how

G **Chorus**

Let My Words Be Few

(I'll Stand in Awe of You)

Words and Music by Matt Redman and Beth Redman

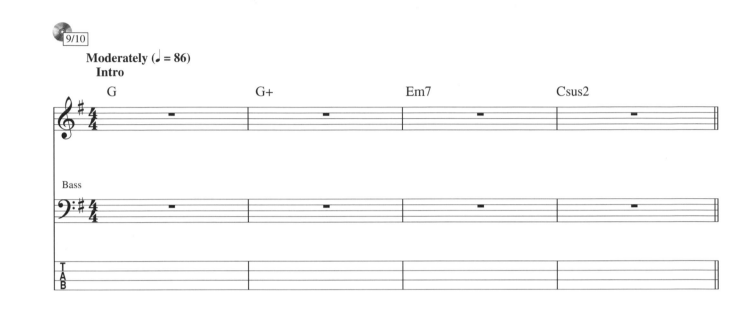

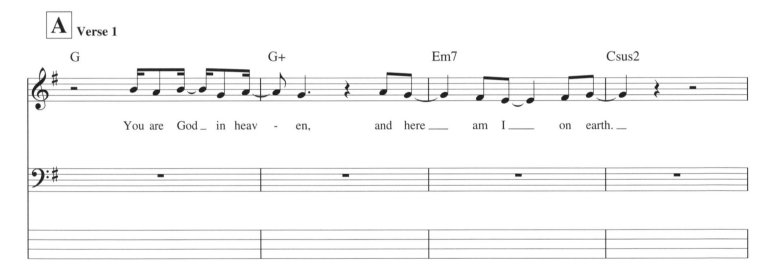

B Chorus

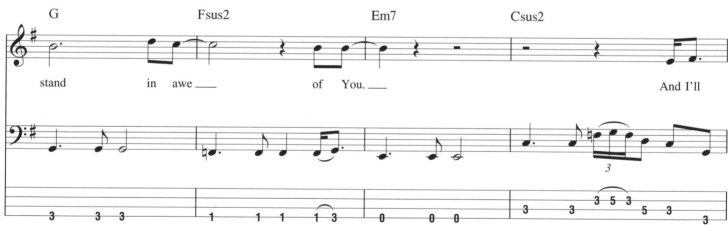

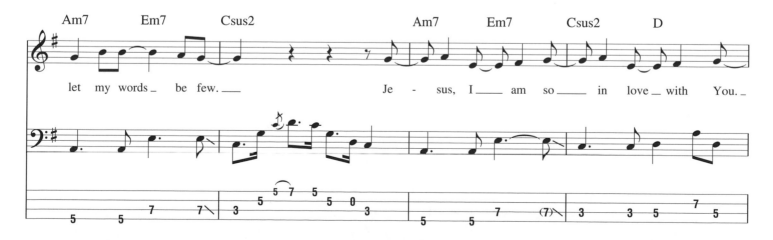

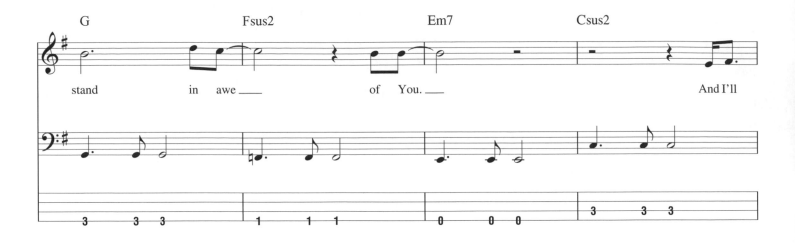

stand in awe ___ of You. ___ And I'll

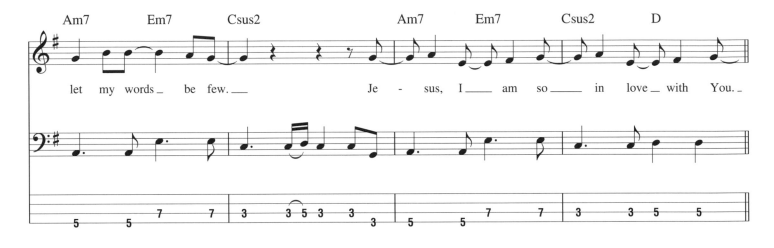

let my words ___ be few. ___ Je - sus, I ___ am so ___ in love ___ with You. ___

F **Tag**

Je - sus, I ___ am so ___ in love ___ with You. ___

Outro

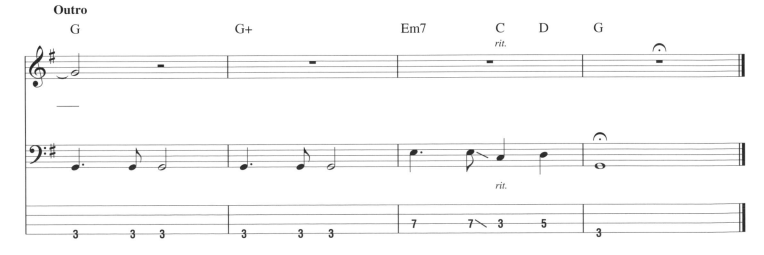

No One Like You

Words and Music by Jack Parker, Mike Dodson, Jason Solley,
Mike Hogan, Jeremy Bush and David Crowder

And ev -'ry day   You're the same,   You nev - er change,   no, nev - er.

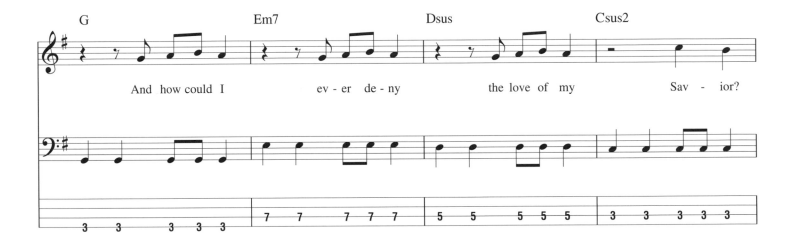

And how could I   ev - er de - ny   the love of my   Sav - ior?

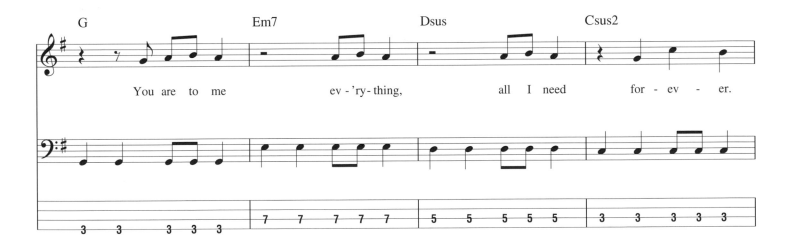

You are to me   ev -'ry- thing,   all I need   for - ev - er.

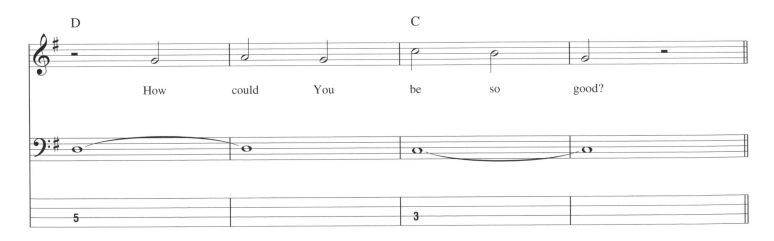

How   could   You   be   so   good?

B **Chorus**

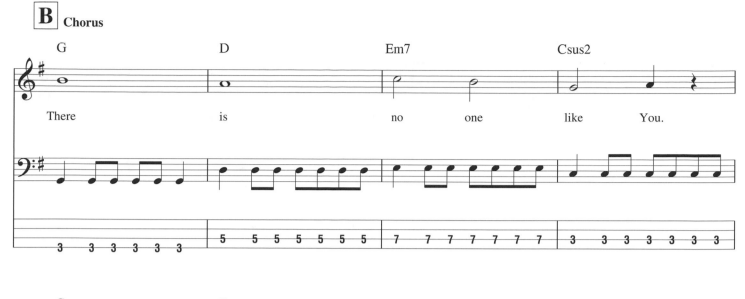

G   D   Em7   Csus2

There   is   no one   like   You.

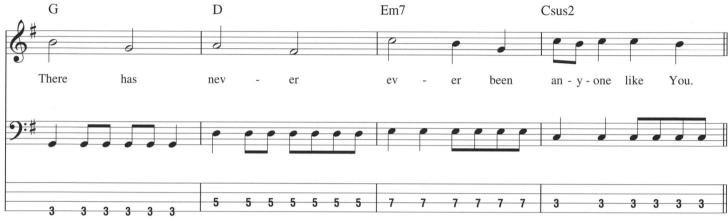

G   D   Em7   Csus2

There   has   nev - er   ev - er been an - y - one like You.

Interlude

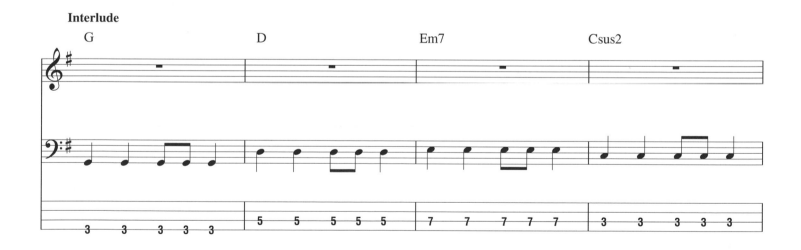

G   D   Em7   Csus2

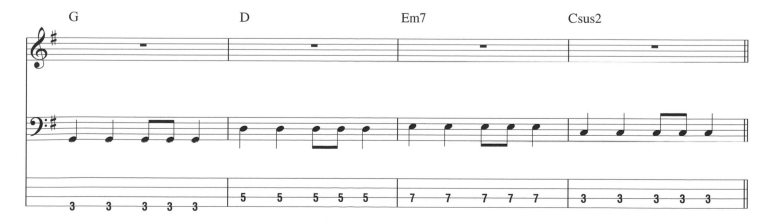

G   D   Em7   Csus2

There has nev - er ev - er been an - y - one like You.

Chorus

There is no one like You.

There has nev - er ev - er been an - y - one like You.

Interlude

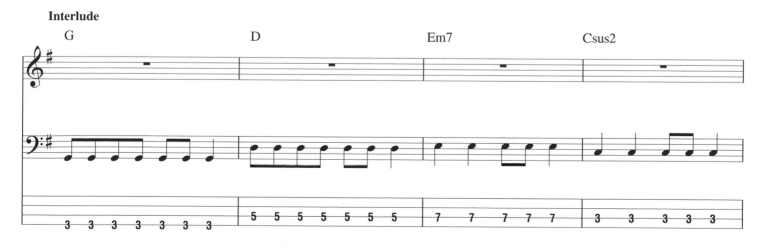

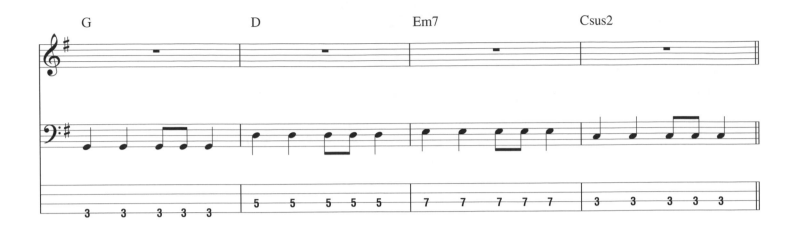

E Bridge

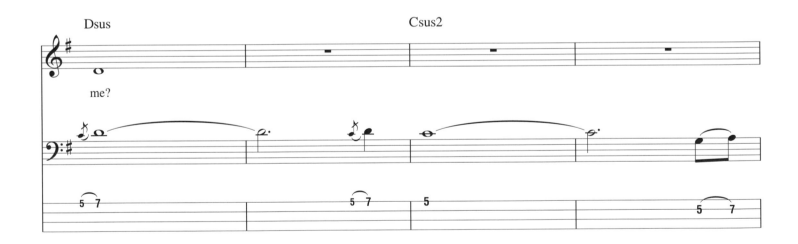

How could You be so good to

me?

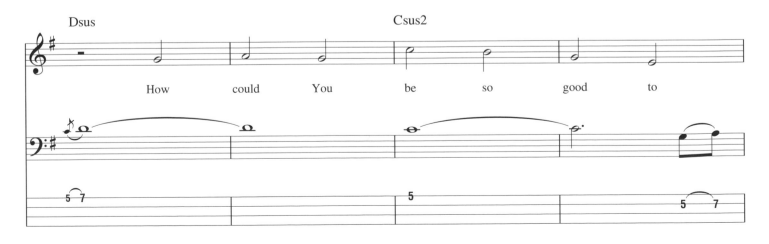

How could You be so good to

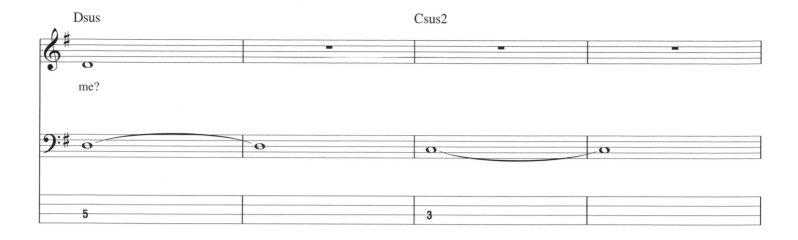

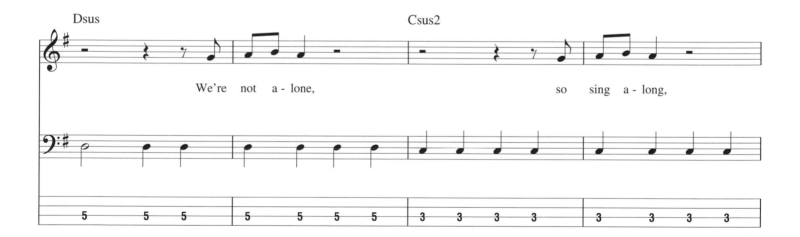

F Chorus

Chorus

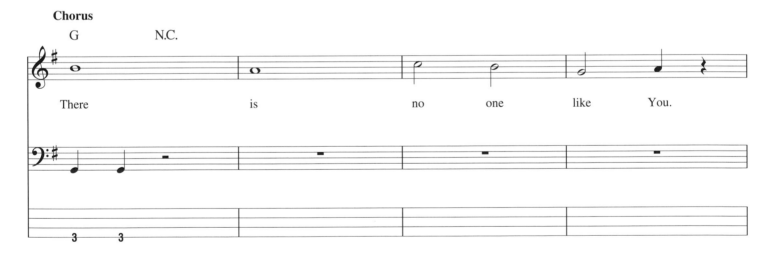

G Chorus

G	D	Em7	Csus2

There is no one like You.

Chorus

G	D	Em7	Csus2

There has nev - er ev - er been an - y - one like You.

G	D	Em7	Csus2

There is no one like You.

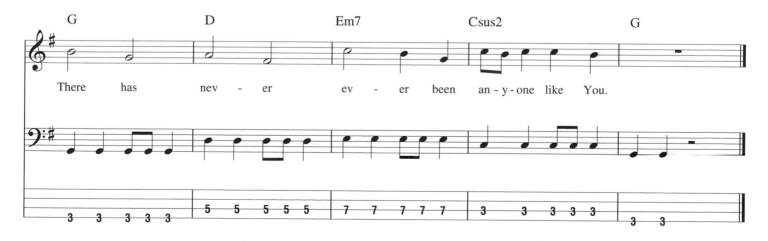

G	D	Em7	Csus2	G

There has nev - er ev - er been an - y - one like You.

Yesterday, Today and Forever

Words and Music by Vicky Beeching

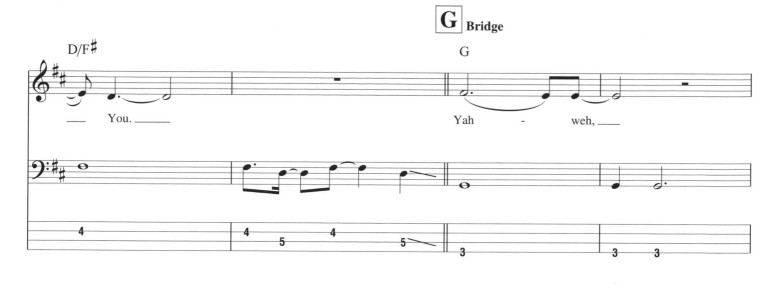

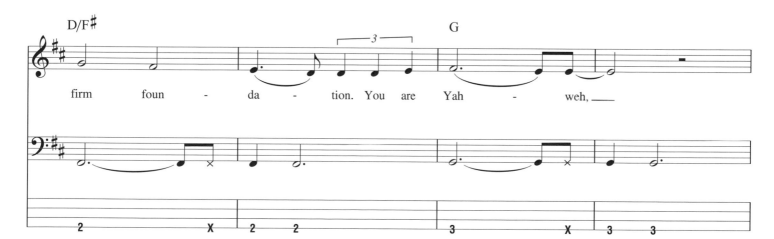

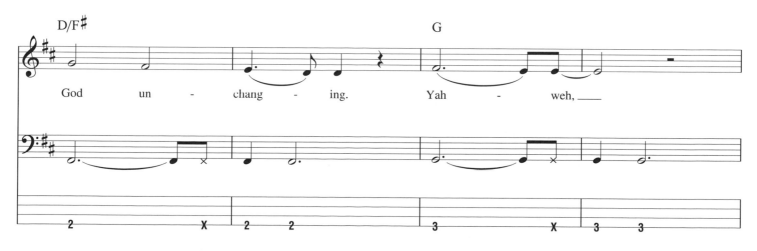

Wonderful Maker

Words and Music by Matt Redman and Chris Tomlin

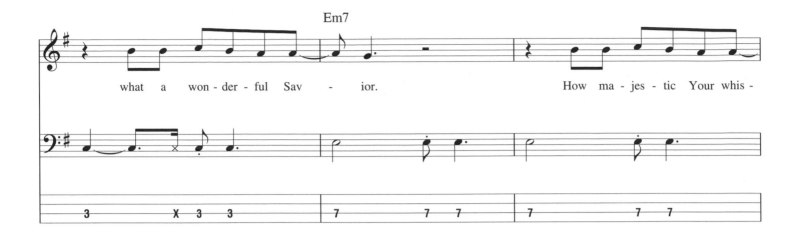

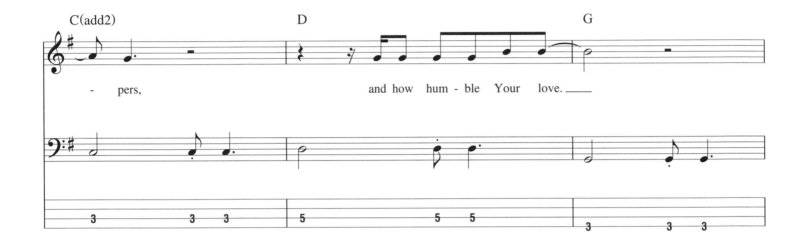

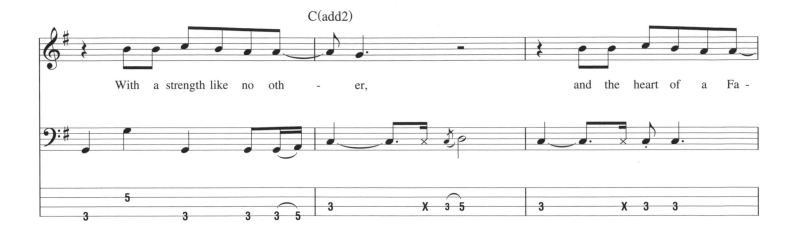

With a strength like no oth - er, and the heart of a Fa -

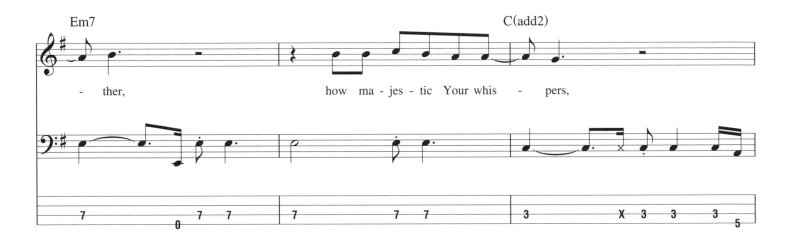

- ther, how ma - jes - tic Your whis - pers,

I Tag

what a won - der - ful _____ God. _____ How ma - jes - tic Your whis - pers,

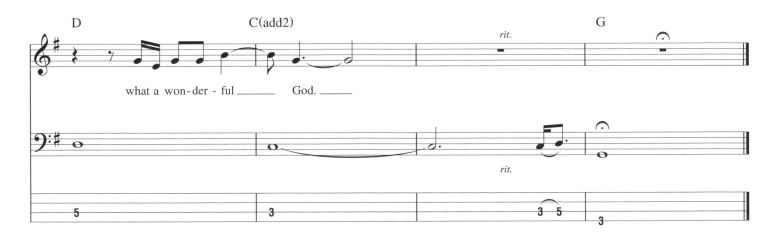

what a won - der - ful _____ God. _____

ABOVE ALL

PAUL BALOCHE and LENNY LeBLANC

Key of **G Major**, 4/4

INTRO:

G G/B C D Em7 D C Dsus D

VERSE:

```
        C      Dsus         G
Above all powers,    above all kings
        C        Dsus       G
Above all nature and all created things
          Em        G/D          C   G/B
Above all wisdom and all the ways of man
Am7                          Dsus  D
You were here before the world began
        C        Dsus       G
Above all kingdoms,    above all thrones
         C        Dsus       G
Above all wonders the world has ever known
          Em        G/D        C   G/B
Above all wealth and treasures of the earth
Am7                              B7
There's no way to measure what You're worth
```

CHORUS:

```
G    Am7  D         G
Crucified,   laid behind a stone
   G    Am7    D        G
You lived to die   rejected and alone
    Em    G/D          C   G/B
Like a rose trampled on the ground
          Am7  G/B             C   Dsus
You took the fall       and thought of me
      G   G/B  C   Dsus  D
Above all  (C/E  D/F♯)
```

(REPEAT VERSE)

(REPEAT CHORUS 2X)

TAG:

```
D/F♯  Em  G/D          C   G/B
Like a rose trampled on the ground
          Am7  G/B             C   Dsus
You took the fall       and thought of me
      G   G/B  C   Dsus  D  G (hold)
Above all
```

BEAUTIFUL SAVIOR (ALL MY DAYS)
STUART TOWNEND

Key of **D Major**, 6/8

INTRO (2X):

Bm7   C6/9   D (2 bars)

VERSE 1:

Bm7   C6/9   D   G/B   C6/9   G
All my days I will sing this song of glad - ness

Bm7   C6/9   D   G/B Csus2
Give my praise to the Fountain of delights

   Am7 Csus2 D   Csus2 G/B   D
For in   my   helplessness, You heard   my   cry

    Am7 Csus2 Bm7   E/G♯   A
And waves   of   mercy poured down on my life

VERSE 2:

Bm7 C6/9   D   G/B   C6/9   G
I will trust in the cross of my Re - deem - er

Bm7 C6/9   D   G/B Csus2
I will sing of the blood that never fails

   Am7 Csus2 D   Csus2 G/B   D
Of sins   for - giv - en, of conscience cleansed

    Am7 Csus2 Bm7   A/C♯ Bm7   A
Of death   de - feated and life without end

CHORUS:

A/G   D/F♯ G   A   A/C♯   D
Beautiful Savior,   Wonderful Coun - sel - or

      Em7   Em7/D
Clothed in majesty, Lord of history

     A/C♯   Bm7   A
You're the Way, the Truth, the Life

A/G   D/F♯   G   A A/C♯   D
Star of the Morning,   glorious in ho - li - ness

    Em7   Em7/D
You're the Risen One, heaven's champion

    A/C♯ Bm7 A   Bm7   C6/9   D (2 bars)
And You reign, You reign (over all)

VERSE 3:

 Bm7 C6/9   D   G/B C6/9   G
I long to be where the praise is never-end - ing

Bm7   C6/9   D   G/B Csus2
Yearn to dwell where the glory never fades

   Am7   Csus2 D   Csus2 G/B   D
Where count - less worshippers will share   one   song

   Am7 Csus2 Bm7   A/C♯ Bm7   A
And cries   of   "Worthy!" will honor the Lamb

(REPEAT CHORUS 2X)

TAG:

Bm7   C6/9   D (2 bars)
(Vocal ad lib.)

DAYS OF ELIJAH

ROBIN MARK

Key of **G Major, 4/4**

INTRO (2X):

G C G D

VERSE 1:

G   C   G   D   G
These are the days of Elijah, declaring the word of the Lord

   G   C   G   D   G
And these are the days of Your servant Moses, righteousness being restored

   Bm   Em   Am   C   Dsus D
And though these are days of great trials, of famine and darkness and sword

   G   C   G   D   G
Still we are the voice in the desert crying, "Prepare ye the way of the Lord!"

CHORUS:

 D   G   C
Behold, He comes, riding on the clouds

            G   D
Shining like the sun at the trumpet call

        G   C
Lift your voice, it's the year of Jubilee

           G   D   G   (C G D)
And out of Zion's hill salvation comes

VERSE 2:

   G   C   G   D   G
And these are the days of Ezekiel, the dry bones becoming as flesh

   G   C   G   D   G
And these are the days of Your servant David, rebuilding a temple of praise

   Bm   Em   Am   C   Dsus D
And these are the days of the harvest, the fields are as white in Your world

   G   C   G   D   G
And we are the laborers in Your vineyard, declaring the word of the Lord

(REPEAT CHORUS 3X)

TAG:

D   G   C
Lift your voice, it's the year of Jubilee

        G   D   G (hold)
And out of Zion's hill salvation comes

HOW GREAT IS OUR GOD

CHRIS TOMLIN, JESSE REEVES and ED CASH

Key of **G Major, 4/4**

INTRO:

G (2 bars)

VERSE 1:

       G   **Em7**
The splendor of the King, clothed in majesty

                Cmaj7
Let all the earth rejoice, all the earth rejoice

   G   **Em7**
He wraps Himself in light, and darkness tries to hide

          Cmaj7
It trembles at His voice, trembles at His voice

CHORUS:

     G
How great is our God. Sing with me

   Em7
How great is our God. All will see

   Cmaj7   **D**   **G**
How great, how great is our God

VERSE 2:

G   **Em7**
Age to age He stands, and time is in His hands

         Cmaj7
Beginning and the End, Beginning and the End

    G   **Em7**
The God-head, Three in One, Father, Spirit, Son

        Cmaj7
The Lion and the Lamb, the Lion and the Lamb

(REPEAT CHORUS)

BRIDGE:

G   **Em7**
Name above all names, worthy of all praise

  Cmaj7   **D**   **G**
My heart will sing: How great is our God!

     G   **Em7**
He's the Name above all names, worthy of all praise

  Cmaj7   **D**   **G**
My heart will sing: How great is our God!

(REPEAT CHORUS 2X)

LET MY WORDS BE FEW (I'LL STAND IN AWE OF YOU)

MATT REDMAN and BETH REDMAN

Key of **G Major, 4/4**

INTRO:

G   G+   Em7   Csus2

VERSE 1:

G   G+   Em7   Csus2
   You are God in heaven, and here am I on earth

G   G+   Em7   Csus2
  So I'll let my words be few

Am7 Em7 Csus2 D   G
Jesus, I am so   in love with You

CHORUS:

       G   Fsus2 Em7 Am7 D7sus
And I'll stand in awe of You

       G   Fsus2 Em7 Csus2
Yes, I'll stand in awe of You

    Am7 Em7   Csus2
And I'll let my words be few

Am7 Em7 Csus2 D   (G)
Jesus, I am so   in love with You

VERSE 2:

G   G+   Em7   Csus2
   The simplest of all love songs I want to bring to You

G   G+   Em7   Csus2
  So I'll let my words be few

Am7 Em7 Csus2 D   G
Jesus, I am so   in love with You

(REPEAT CHORUS 2X)

TAG:

Am7 Em7   Csus2

Am7 Em7   Csus2 D
Jesus, I am so   in love with You

OUTRO:

G G+ Em7 C D G (hold)

NO ONE LIKE YOU

JACK PARKER, MIKE DODSON, JASON SOLLEY, MIKE HOGAN, JEREMY BUSH and DAVID CROWDER

Key of **G Major**, 4/4

INTRO (2X):

G   D   Em7   Csus2

VERSE 1:

G   Em7   Dsus   Csus2
You are more   beautiful   than anyone   ever

G   Em7   Dsus   Csus2
And ev'ry day   You're the same,   You never change,   no, never

G   Em7   Dsus   Csus2
And how could I   ever deny   the love of my   Savior?

G   Em7   Dsus   Csus2
You are to me   ev'rything,   all I need   forever

D   C
How could You be so good?

CHORUS:

G   D Em7 Csus2
There is   no one like You

G   D Em7   Csus2
There has never ever been anyone like You

INTERLUDE (2X):

G   D   Em7   Csus2

VERSE 2:

G   Em7   Dsus   Csus2
Ev'rywhere,   You are there,   earth or air,   surrounding

G   Em7   Dsus   Csus2
I'm not alone,   the heavens sing along.   My God, You're so   astounding

G   Em7   Dsus   Csus2
How could You be   so good to me?   Eternally, I believe

(REPEAT CHORUS 2X)

(REPEAT INTERLUDE)

BRIDGE:

Dsus   Csus2   Dsus   Csus2
How could You be so good to me?

Dsus   Csus2   Dsus   Csus2
How could You be so good to me?

Dsus   Csus2
We're not alone,   so sing along

Dsus   Csus2
We're not alone,   so sing along, sing along, sing along

(REPEAT CHORUS 4X)

END ON G

WONDERFUL MAKER

MATT REDMAN and CHRIS TOMLIN

Key of **G Major**, 4/4

INTRO:

G/B C(add2)   Em7   G/B

VERSE 1:

C(add2)
You spread out the skies over empty space

Em7   C(add2)   D/F♯   G/B
Said, "Let there be light;" to a dark and formless world Your light was born

VERSE 2:

C(add2)
You spread out Your arms over empty hearts

Em7   C(add2)   D
Said, "Let there be light;" to a dark and hopeless world Your Son was born

PRE-CHORUS:

   Am7   G/B   C(add2)
You made the world and saw that it was good

   Am7   G/B   C(add2)   D/F♯
You sent Your only Son, for You are good

CHORUS:

                     C(add2)   Em7
What a wonderful Maker, what a wonderful Savior

                     C(add2)   D   G
How majestic Your whispers,   and how humble Your love

                     C(add2)   Em7
With a strength like no other, and the heart of a Father

                     C(add2)   D   G
How majestic Your whispers,   what a wonderful God

VERSE 3:

   C(add2)
No eye has fully seen how beautiful the cross

   Em7   C(add2)   D
And we have only heard the faintest whispers of how great You are

(REPEAT PRE-CHORUS)

(REPEAT CHORUS 2X)

TAG:

(G)   C(add2)   D   C(add2)   G (hold)
How majestic Your whispers,   what a wonderful God

YESTERDAY, TODAY AND FOREVER

VICKY BEECHING

Key of **D Major**, 4/4

INTRO:

D/F♯ G   Bm7 A

D/F♯ G   Bm7 A

VERSE 1:

G   Bm7
Everlasting God

    G   Bm7
The years go by, but You're unchanging

G   Bm7
In this fragile world

     G   Bm7
You are the only firm foundation

Em7   D/F♯
   Always loving, always true

G   Bm7   A
   Always merciful and good, so good

CHORUS:

D/F♯   G   Bm7   A
Yesterday, today and forever

D/F♯   G   Bm7   A
You are the same, You never change

D/F♯ G   Bm7   A
Yesterday, today and forever

Em7   G   A
You are faithful and we will trust in You

(REPEAT INTRO) – *Vocal ad lib.*

VERSE 2:

G   Bm7
Uncreated One

    G   Bm7
You have no end and no beginning

G   Bm7
Earthly powers fade

     G   Bm7
But there is no end to Your Kingdom

Em7   D/F♯
   Always loving, always true

G   Bm7   A
   Always merciful and good, so good

(REPEAT CHORUS 2X)

INTERLUDE:

G   D/F♯   G   D/F♯
(Vocal ad lib.)

BRIDGE:

G   D/F♯
Yahweh, God unchanging

G   D/F♯
Yahweh, firm foundation. You are

G   D/F♯
Yahweh, God unchanging

G   D/F♯
Yahweh, firm foundation

(REPEAT CHORUS 2X)

OUTRO (4X):

D/F♯ G   Bm7 A
(Vocal ad lib.)

END ON D